D1544915

EXPLORING COUNTRIES

Scotland

by Derek Zobel

BELLWETHER MEDIA · MINNEAPOLIS, MN

Note to Librarians, Teachers, and Parents:

Blastoff! Readers are carefully developed by literacy experts and combine standards-based content with developmentally appropriate text.

Level 1 provides the most support through repetition of high-frequency words, light text, predictable sentence patterns, and strong visual support.

Level 2 offers early readers a bit more challenge through varied simple sentences, increased text load, and less repetition of high-frequency words.

Level 3 advances early-fluent readers toward fluency through increased text and concept load, less reliance on visuals, longer sentences, and more literary language.

Level 4 builds reading stamina by providing more text per page, increased use of punctuation, greater variation in sentence patterns, and increasingly challenging vocabulary.

Level 5 encourages children to move from "learning to read" to "reading to learn" by providing even more text, varied writing styles, and less familiar topics.

Whichever book is right for your reader, Blastoff! Readers are the perfect books to build confidence and encourage a love of reading that will last a lifetime!

This edition first published in 2012 by Bellwether Media, Inc.

No part of this publication may be reproduced in whole or in part without written permission of the publisher. For information regarding permission, write to Bellwether Media, Inc., Attention: Permissions Department, 5357 Penn Avenue South, Minneapolis, MN 55419.

Library of Congress Cataloging-in-Publication Data
Zobel, Derek, 1983-
Scotland / by Derek Zobel.
   p. cm. – (Blastoff! readers–exploring countries)
Includes bibliographical references and index.
Summary: "Developed by literacy experts for students in grades three through seven, this book introduces young readers to the geography and culture of Scotland"–Provided by publisher.
ISBN 978-1-60014-734-0 (hardcover : alk. paper)
1. Scotland–Juvenile literature. 2. Scotland–Social life and customs–Juvenile literature. I. Title.
DA762.Z63 2012
941.1–dc23   2011034781

Printed in the United States of America, North Mankato, MN.

010112   1203

Contents

Where Is Scotland?

Orkney Islands

Did you know?

The Orkney Islands lie off the northern coast of Scotland. They have ruins of civilizations from thousands of years ago!

Scotland

Edinburgh

Atlantic Ocean

Northern Ireland

Irish Sea

England

Wales

N

W E

S

Scotland is a country that covers the northern part of **Great Britain** and includes several small islands. It spans a total of 30,414 square miles (78,772 square kilometers). Together with England, Wales, and Northern Ireland, it makes up the **United Kingdom (U.K.)**.

The Atlantic Ocean lies to the north and west of Scotland. The Irish Sea is to the southwest, and to the east lies the North Sea. Scotland's capital, Edinburgh, is located on the eastern coast. Scotland shares its southern border with England.

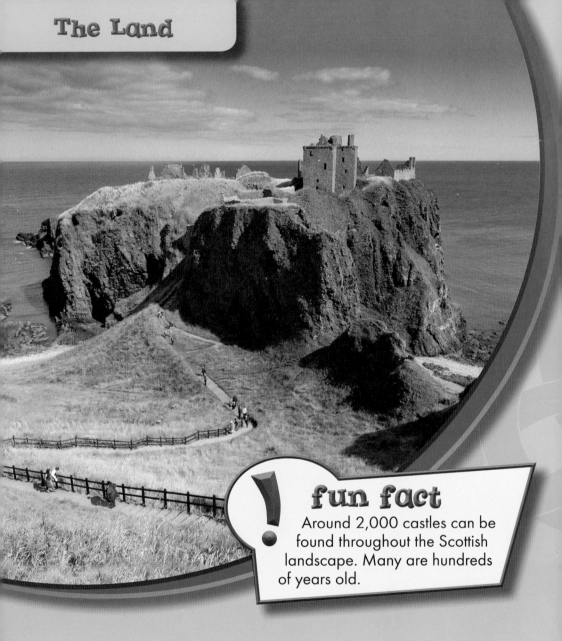

fun fact

Around 2,000 castles can be found throughout the Scottish landscape. Many are hundreds of years old.

Scotland has a variety of landscapes. Many **fjords** cut into the coasts. The Scottish call these *firths*, and the four largest are Moray, Lorne, Solway, and Clyde. On the western part of the country, many islands lie near or within the *firths* and farther off the coasts.

In the north, the highlands consist of peaks, cliffs, and steep valleys. Ben Nevis is the highest point in all of Great Britain. It rises 4,406 feet (1,343 meters) in the highlands. The middle of Scotland contains sweeping hills and is lower than the highlands. To the south, the landscape rises before gently meeting the sea.

Did you know?
Scottish people from the highlands are called highlanders. Those from the lowlands are called lowlanders.

Loch Ness holds more water than any other lake in Great Britain. Located in the Great Glen of the highlands, it has a depth of 788 feet (240 meters). The water level rises and falls often, and the shores quickly give way to deep waters. For these reasons, little plant life can survive in the lake.

Loch Ness Monster

According to legend, Loch Ness is home to a sea monster that became trapped when the lake closed off from the ocean. Some people believe the murky water keeps it hidden from view. People have taken photographs and videos of what they claim to be the creature!

Atlantic seal

The landscapes of Scotland support many kinds of wildlife. Roe, red, and fallow deer are plentiful in the forests and plains. These areas are also home to pine martens, foxes, badgers, and hares. Above them, hungry eagles, falcons, and kestrels fly in circles searching for prey.

Did you know?

Every year, Atlantic seals gather along Scotland's western coast. About half of all Atlantic seals in the world breed in these waters.

badger

fallow deer

peregrine falcon

fun fact

The peregrine falcon is found throughout Scotland. When it dives at prey, it can reach a speed of 200 miles (320 kilometers) per hour!

The waters off the coasts of Scotland contain fish, seals, and whales. Dolphins and porpoises can be seen leaping from the sea. Along the coasts, gulls, fulmars, gannets, and other seabirds fly in search of their next meal.

Did you know?

The peoples of the Shetland and Orkney Islands trace their heritage to the Norse. These are Scandinavians who settled the islands over 1,000 years ago.

Most Scottish people trace their heritage back to either the **Celts** or the **Anglo-Saxons**. The Celts are the **ancestors** of the Scots from the highlands. Scots from the lowlands are **descendants** of Anglo-Saxons. Scotland is also home to many Irish. They have come across the Irish Sea in search of work. Many people from other European countries also live in Scotland. Recently, **immigrants** have come to Scotland from countries in Asia. Most Scots speak English, but a few still speak Scottish Gaelic. The government has made efforts to preserve this old language.

Speak Scottish Gaelic!

English	Scottish Gaelic	How to say it
hello	halò	HAH-loh
good-bye	mar sin leibh	mahr sin LEH-eev
yes	tha	HAH
no	chan eil	han yale
please	ma 's e ur toil e	mah sheh oor TUL-leh
thank you	tapadh leibh	TAH-puh LEH-eev
friend	caraid	CAH-ritsh

Did you know?

Most neighborhoods have public houses where Scots gather in the evening to chat with friends.

In the past, Scots lived mainly in the countryside. Today, most live in houses and apartments in large cities. They buy goods in supermarkets, malls, and small shops. Some Scots still live in the countryside. They live in houses and shop at markets in small villages.

Train tracks and a large **network** of roads allow people to move throughout Scotland. In cities, many people take buses to get around town. If Scots want to travel to an island, they can fly or take a **ferry**.

Where People Live in Scotland

countryside 39%

cities 61%

Most Scottish children start their education in preschool. All children must attend school from ages 5 to 16. They can attend public school for free or pay to go to private school. Primary school begins at age 5 and lasts for seven years. Secondary school follows, and students must attend for four years. Some students stay longer.

Throughout their schooling, young Scots study science, math, art, social studies, music, and physical education. Students are taught Scottish Gaelic in regions where the language is common. After finishing secondary school, many Scots go on to study at universities or **vocational schools**.

fun fact

Founded in 1413, the University of St. Andrews is the oldest university in Scotland. Royalty have attended this university.

Where People Work in Scotland

manufacturing 20%

services 78%

farming 2%

Most Scots have **service jobs**. This includes
jobs at banks, hospitals, schools, and government
offices. Workers at restaurants, hotels, and museums
serve more than one million **tourists** who come to
Scotland every year. Some Scots work in factories that
make electronics, clothing, and other goods. These
items are shipped around the world from Scotland's
many **ports**. Off the coasts, fishers cast their nets into
the sea. Scotland has access to oil in the North Sea,
and **oil platforms** keep workers busy year-round.

shinty

Soccer and **rugby** are the most popular sports in
Scotland. The country has a national team for each
sport. Golf is also popular throughout the country.
The British Open, one of the four major tournaments
in golf, is often held in Scotland. *Shinty*, a sport that
originated in Scotland, is like field hockey. Each team
uses long sticks to hit a ball into the other team's goal.

The Scottish landscape is ideal for many outdoor activities. Hikers and climbers hit the highlands during all seasons. People sail and canoe along the coasts and in lakes and rivers. They share the waters with the thousands of Scots who enjoy fishing.

fun fact

Many Scots also participate in curling, a sport where large, smooth stones are slid across ice toward a target.

Did you know?

In Scotland, fish-and-chips is a meal of fried fish and French fries. Street vendors often serve this meal to customers in wrapped newspaper!

Scottish food is simple and uses very few spices. Many Scots start the day with porridge. They often top it with berries. **Hearty** soups are enjoyed for both lunch and dinner. Scotch broth is a combination of barley, lamb meat, carrots, turnips, and other vegetables. *Cock-a-leekie* soup is made of chicken and **leeks** cooked in chicken broth. Some Scots add prunes for a hint of sweetness. The most famous Scottish dish is *haggis*. To make it, people cut up the lungs, liver, and heart of a sheep. They **mince** the organs with onions, oats, salt, and pepper. The mixture is then stuffed into the sheep's stomach and boiled for a few hours.

fun fact

Shortbread originated in Scotland. This buttery treat is often served with tea or coffee for a snack.

haggis

Did you know?

The Glasgow Fair is an 800-year-old tradition that takes place during the last two weeks of July. People take time off work to vacation or enjoy the fair events.

St. Andrew's Day

Scotland's national holiday is St. Andrew's Day, which falls on November 30. This day celebrates St. Andrew, the **patron saint** of Scotland. Scottish people celebrate the New Year with a custom called "first-footing." They try to be the first to visit their friends and family in the early morning on New Year's Day. It is tradition for the visitors to bring gifts of shortbread, coal, and spiced cakes.

Most Scots also celebrate Christmas and Easter. For Christmas, Scots gather with their families to give gifts, feast on traditional foods, and decorate their houses. On Easter, families enjoy a large meal that usually includes roast lamb.

caber toss

! fun fact

When participating in the caber toss and hammer throw, a man must wear a kilt. This traditional piece of Scottish clothing is knee-length, pleated, and plaid.

Scotland has many cultural traditions surrounding sports and competition. The **Highland Games** originated in the highlands hundreds of years ago. Two famous events are the caber toss and the hammer throw. In the caber toss, a Scot carries a tree trunk vertically before hurling it, end over end, as far as possible. A caber weighs around 90 pounds (40 kilograms) and is about 17 feet (5 meters) long! In the hammer throw, a Scot holds a hammer with a wooden or wire handle and an iron ball for a head. He swings the hammer to build up speed before releasing it into the air. The Highland Games are accompanied by traditional Scottish music and dance. They are a celebration of all that it means to be a Scot!

Fast Facts About Scotland

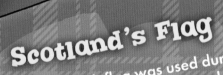

Scotland's Flag

The current Scottish flag was used during wars with England for independence and remains a symbol of Scottish patriotism today. The X-shaped cross is the symbol of St. Andrew, the patron saint of Scotland. The flag was officially adopted sometime in the 1500s.

Official Name: Scotland

Area: 30,414 square miles (78,772 square kilometers); Scotland is the 2ND largest country in the United Kingdom.

Capital City:	Edinburgh
Important Cities:	Glasgow, Aberdeen, Dundee
Population:	5,222,100 (July 2010)
Official Language:	English
National Holiday:	St. Andrew's Day (November 30)
Religions:	Christian (65%), None (33%), Other (2%)
Major Industries:	farming, fishing, manufacturing, services
Natural Resources:	coal, timber, hydroelectric power, oil, zinc
Manufactured Products:	electronics, clothing, ships, food products, transportation equipment
Farm Products:	wheat, oats, potatoes, barley, berries, mutton, beef, dairy products
Unit of Money:	pound sterling; the pound is divided into 100 pence.

Glossary

ancestors—relatives who lived long ago

Anglo-Saxons—a people group that came from parts of Europe around Germany and settled in England

Celts—a people group that came from central Europe and settled in Scotland and Scandinavia

descendants—younger family members who are all related to one older family member

ferry—a boat or ship used to carry passengers across a body of water

fjords—long, narrow inlets of the ocean between tall cliffs; the movement of glaciers makes fjords.

Great Britain—an island off the northwest coast of Europe; England, Scotland, and Wales make up Great Britain.

hearty—filling and comforting

Highland Games—traditional Scottish games which originated in the highlands of Scotland hundreds of years ago

immigrants—people who leave one country to live in another country

leeks—vegetables similar to onions

mince—to chop into very small pieces

network—a group of connected objects

oil platforms—large structures at sea from which workers drill for oil

patron saint—a saint who is believed to look after a country or group of people

ports—sea harbors where ships can dock; ships from around the world deliver and pick up goods in Scotland's ports.

rugby—a team sport played with a ball that may be thrown backward, kicked, or carried

service jobs—jobs that perform tasks for people or businesses

tourists—people who are visiting a country

United Kingdom (U.K.)—a nation that includes England, Scotland, Wales, and Northern Ireland

vocational schools—schools that train students to do specific jobs

To Learn More

AT THE LIBRARY

Brassey, Richard, and Stewart Ross. *The Story of Scotland*. London, U.K.: Orion Children's Books, 1999.

Waldron, Melanie. *Scotland*. Chicago, Ill.: Heinemann Library, 2012.

Wilson, Barbara Ker. *Stories from Scotland*. Oxford, U.K.: Oxford University Press, 2009.

ON THE WEB

Learning more about Scotland is as easy as 1, 2, 3.

1. Go to www.factsurfer.com.

2. Enter "Scotland" into the search box.

3. Click the "Surf" button and you will see a list of related Web sites.

With factsurfer.com, finding more information is just a click away.

Index